CONNECT BIBLE STUDIES

Friends

Warner Bros.

www.connectbiblestudies.com

connect
linking the Word to the world

CONNECT BIBLE STUDIES: Friends

Published in this format by Scripture Union, 207–209 Queensway, Bletchley, MK2 2EB, England.

Scripture Union is an international Christian charity working with churches in more than 130 countries providing resources to bring the good news about Jesus Christ to children, young people and families – and to encourage them to develop spiritually through the Bible and prayer. As well as a network of volunteers, staff and associates who run holidays, church-based events and school Christian groups, Scripture Union produces a wide range of publications and supports those who use the resources through training programmes.

Email: info@scriptureunion.org.uk
Internet: www.scriptureunion.org.uk

© Damaris Trust, PO Box 200, Southampton, SO17 2DL

Damaris Trust enables people to relate Christian faith and contemporary culture. It helps them to think about issues within society from a Christian perspective and explore God's truth as it is revealed in the Bible. Damaris provides resources via the Internet, workshops, publications and products.

Email: office@damaris.org
Internet: www.damaris.org

British Library Cataloguing-in-Publication Data: a catalogue record for this book is available from the British Library.

First published 2003 ISBN 1 85999 775 9

ALSO AVAILABLE AS AN ELECTRONIC DOWNLOAD: www.connectbiblestudies.com

Damaris writers: Di Archer, Caroline Puntis, Tony Watkins
SU editors: Lin Ball, Andrew Clark

Cover design by aricot vert of Fleet, UK.

Cover photo from European Press Agency/ PA Photos Ltd shows Jennifer Aniston, David Schwimmer and Lisa Kudrow of Friends, holding their People's Choice Award for Favourite TV Comedy series at the ceremony in Jan 2001, Pasadena, California.

Print production by CPO, Garcia Estate, Canterbury Road, Worthing, West Sussex BN13 1BW.

CPO is a Christian publishing charity working in partnership with over 30,000 churches and other Christian organizations worldwide, using the power of design and print to convey the message of Jesus Christ. Established for over 45 years, CPO is the UK's premier supplier of publicity and related resources to the UK Church, available through a direct mail catalogue series, an e-commerce website and most Christian bookshops.

Email:connect@cpo.org.uk
Internet:www.cpo-online.org

Other titles in this series:

And more titles following. Check www.connectbiblestudies.com for latest titles or ask at any good Christian bookshop.

Using Connect Bible Studies

What are these studies?

These innovative small group Bible studies have two aims. Firstly, to enable people to dig into their Bibles and get to know them better. Secondly, by being based on contemporary films, books, TV programmes etc, the aim is to help people think through topical issues in a Biblical way.

It is not envisaged that all the group will always be able to watch the films or read the books, or indeed that they will always want to. A summary is always provided. However, our vision is that knowing about these films and books empowers Christians engage with friends and colleagues about them. Addressing issues from a Biblical perspective gives Christians confidence that they know what they think, and can bring a distinctive angle to bear in conversations.

The studies are each produced with four weeks' worth of group material. These are available in print, published by Scripture Union, from your local Christian bookshop, or via the Internet at www.connectbiblestudies.com. Anyone can sign up for a free email newsletter that announces the new studies and provides other information: www.connectbiblestudies.com/register

How do I use them?

The studies are designed to stimulate creative thought and discussion within a Biblical context. Each section has a range of questions or options from which the leader may choose in order to tailor the study to your group's needs and desires. Different approaches may appeal at different times, so the studies aim to supply choice.

Group members should all be supplied with the appropriate sheet to fill in – either by having their own copy of the booklet, or by having a photocopy of the Members' Sheet which follows each study session.

Leader's notes contain:

1. Opening questions

These help your group settle in to discussion, while introducing the topics. They may be straightforward, personal or creative, but aim to provoke a response.

2. Summary

We suggest the summary of the book or film will follow now, read aloud if necessary. There may well be reactions that group members want to express even before getting on to the week's issue.

3. Key issue

Again, either read from the leader's notes, or summarise.

4. Bible study

Lots of choice here. Choose as appropriate to suit your group – get digging into the Bible. Background reading and texts for further help and study are suggested, but please use the material provided to inspire your group to explore their Bibles as much as possible. A concordance might be a handy standby for looking things up. A commentary could be useful too, such as the *New Bible Commentary* 21st century edition (IVP, 1994). The idea is to help people to engage with the truth of God's word, wrestling with it if necessary but making it their own.

Don't plan to work through every question here. Within each section the two questions explore roughly the same ground but from different angles or in different ways. Our advice is to take one question from each section. The questions are open-ended so each ought to yield good discussion – though of course any discussion in a Bible study may need prompting to go a little further.

5. Implications

Here the aim is to tie together the perspectives gained through Bible study and the impact of the book or film. The implications may be personal, a change in worldview, or new ideas for relating to non-churchgoers. Choose questions that adapt to the flow of the discussion.

6. Prayer

Leave time for it! We suggest a time of open prayer, or praying in pairs if the group would prefer. Encourage your members to focus on issues from your study that had a particular impact on them. Try different approaches to prayer – light a candle, say a prayer each, write prayers down, play quiet worship music – aiming to facilitate everyone to relate to God.

7. Background reading

You will find links to some background reading on the Connect Bible Studies website: www.connectbiblestudies.com

8. Online discussion

You can discuss the studies online with others on the Connect Bible Studies website at www.connectbiblestudies.com

linking the Word to the world

Friends

Warner Bros.

Part One: Selfishness

Phoebe:	*Where is everyone? They're forty minutes late.*
Joey:	*I know.*
Phoebe:	*I'm starving. I knew we were coming here tonight, so I ate nothing all day.*
Joey:	*What about me, huh? Only had one lunch today.*

Please read Using Connect Bible Studies *(page 3) before leading a Bible study using this material.*

Opening Questions

Choose one of these questions.

How would you define selfishness?	Do you think the characters in *Friends* are selfish? Why/why not?
When do you behave selfishly?	Is it ever right to put yourself first? Why/why not?

Summary

Friends is ultimately the story of six self-centred people who occasionally think about one another. Rarely is there any display of self-sacrifice or putting someone else's needs first. The irony produced is the basis for much of the humour that makes the series so entertaining.

Apart from the sibling bond between Ross and Monica, the relationships have taken some time to grow. By the ninth series, the attachments in the group are well established – Ross and Rachel live together, have a baby together, but are not 'together'. Chandler and Monica are married. Phoebe has found love for the first time. In spite of these ties, the search for personal happiness is still very high on everyone's agenda. When Chandler is forced to move to Tulsa with his job

(*The One With the Paediatrician*), Monica decides that she will go with him – until she is offered the job of a lifetime in New York. Without even bothering to consult her husband, she agrees to take the position.

In *The One With Phoebe's Birthday Dinner*, Phoebe and Joey wait impatiently in an expensive restaurant for Monica, Chandler, Rachel and Ross. When the two couples finally arrive, they selfishly bring their own concerns to the dinner table. Phoebe's frustration with her friends makes her unrepentant when her boyfriend calls her away. Relieved, the latecomers make a hasty departure. Joey, preoccupied throughout the episode with his hunger, finally gets to eat in an unparalleled show of greed: 'Dinner for six – for one!'

Key Issue: Selfishness

The American sitcom *Friends* has become extraordinarily popular, and in our studies we look at some of the underlying themes which make it so attractive. While entertaining us with irresistible humour, it would be hard to deny that the six friends lead essentially selfish lives. They pursue their own individual desires, and 'do their own thing'. And it all looks such fun. So what does the Bible say about selfishness? Is there really anything wrong with it? How does it affect us and our communities? Does it actually matter whether we put ourselves or God first?

Bible Study

Choose one question from each section. One question in each section is based on James 4 and you may wish to follow these through.

1. What is selfishness?

It's my first birthday with a boyfriend, and he has to work. Ugh, I get mad at him, but I think it's a little too soon to show my true colours. (Phoebe)

◆ Read Ezekiel 28:1–10. Why did the king of Tyre think he could do whatever he liked? What was God's verdict about him?

◆ Read James 4:1–17. Why are we selfish? How does it affect our relationship with God?

2. Me first

Chandler: *Alright, look. I don't smoke anymore. But if the rest of you want to light up, go ahead, it's fine ... So you all smoke then? That's almost rude, that I'm not.*
Ken: *That's not true. If you don't wanna smoke ...*
Chandler: *Ken, please! No, I can't, I can't smoke. If I smoke, my wife would kill me.*
Ken: *I'm sorry, but isn't your wife back in New York?*
Chandler: *I always liked you, Ken.*

◆ Read Acts 5:1–11. What were the underlying attitudes of Ananias and Sapphira? Why did they think they could get away with it?

◆ Read James 4:1–17. What does selfishness make us do? What are the results?

3. Me at all costs

Chandler: *But you said you forgave me ...*
Monica: *I was just saying that because I was ovulating and you said you wouldn't have sex with me while we're fighting.*
Chandler: *You tricked me to get me into bed?*
Monica: *That's right, I got mine.*
Chandler: *I feel so used!*

◆ Read Genesis 37:1–36. What led Joseph's brothers to act this way? How did this impact the whole family?

◆ Read James 4:1–17. How does selfishness impact others?

4. Me and God

Look, I know, you all have a lot going on, but all I wanted to do was have dinner with my friends on my birthday. And you are all so late and you didn't even have the courtesy to call. (Phoebe)

◆ Read Luke 6:27–36. Why is it not enough to 'love those who love you'? Why does Jesus want us to act in such a revolutionary way?

◆ Read James 4:1–17. How does God want us to relate to him and to others?

Implications

Rachel: *Phoebe, we're so sorry. You're totally right. We are here one hundred per cent and we love you and we are ready to start your birthday celebration ...*
Phoebe: *Oh, I love you guys too, but Mike got off work early. Wait. Wait, I'm not the kind of girl that just ditches her friends to be with her boyfriend. You know what? I am! Bye guys!*

Choose one or more of the following questions.

◆ How does selfishness in others affect you? How does your selfishness affect others?

◆ Who are the people you find it hard to love? How can knowing Jesus help you?

◆ Do you ask God for what you want? Why/why not?

- How might your relationship to God free you from the need to be selfish? How can you realise the truth of this more?

- Though we may not immediately face the kind of fatal judgement that Ananias and Sapphira did, God does see all our actions, and knows our thoughts. Do you have things you need to sort out with him?

- What would you say to someone who says he has to put himself first, because nobody else will?

- What would you say to someone who thinks the *Friends* selfish lifestyle is the way to be?

Prayer

Spend some time praying through these issues.

Background Reading

You will find links to some background reading on the Connect Bible Studies website: www.connectbiblestudies.com

Discuss

Discuss this study in the online discussion forums at www.connectbiblestudies.com

Members' Sheet: Friends – Part 1
Summary

Friends is ultimately the story of six self-centred people who occasionally think about one another. Rarely is there any display of self-sacrifice or putting someone else's needs first. The irony produced is the basis for much of the humour that makes the series so entertaining.

Apart from the sibling bond between Ross and Monica, the relationships have taken some time to grow. By the ninth series, the attachments in the group are well established – Ross and Rachel live together, have a baby together, but are not 'together'. Chandler and Monica are married. Phoebe has found love for the first time. In spite of these ties, the search for personal happiness is still very high on everyone's agenda. When Chandler is forced to move to Tulsa with his job (*The One With the Paediatrician*), Monica decides that she will go with him – until she is offered the job of a lifetime in New York. Without even bothering to consult her husband, she agrees to take the position.

In *The One With Phoebe's Birthday Dinner*, Phoebe and Joey wait impatiently in an expensive restaurant for Monica, Chandler, Rachel and Ross. When the two couples finally arrive, they selfishly bring their own concerns to the dinner table. Phoebe's frustration with her friends makes her unrepentant when her boyfriend calls her away. Relieved, the latecomers make a hasty departure. Joey, preoccupied throughout the episode with his hunger, finally gets to eat in an unparalleled show of greed: 'Dinner for six – for one!'

Key Issue

Bible Study notes

Implications

Prayer

Discuss this study in the online discussion forums at www.connectbiblestudies.com

linking the Word to the world

Friends

Warner Bros.

Part Two: Living in the City

Joey: **What do you guys know about investments?**
Chandler: **How come?**
Joey: **Well, I'm starting to make good money on the show and I'm thinking ... I should probably do something with it.**
Monica: **What do you do with your money now?**
Joey: **Well, I just tape it to the back of my toilet tank. I didn't say that! It's in a bank guarded by robots!**

Please read Using Connect Bible Studies *(page 3) before leading a Bible study using this material.*

Opening Questions

Choose one of these questions.

Do you find city life attractive? Why/why not?	What do you think are the best and worst things about living in the city?
Would *Friends* work if set in the countryside? Why/why not?	What is your favourite city and why?

Summary

New York – the ultimate high-rise, high-living city. Somewhere in Manhattan there is a corner that is home to six friends. They all have their own reasons for ending up in the city, but share a love for the place that has offered them so much. New York has got room for Ross the palaeontologist, Phoebe the masseuse, Joey the actor – and there is always opportunity for growth. Rachel transformed herself from a waitress into a fashion industry executive. When she first arrived in New York, Rachel couldn't even do her own washing. Over the last ten years her confidence has grown and now she is the independent woman of her dreams.

Most of the action takes place in or between the 'Central Perk' coffee house and Monica's apartment, which she now shares with husband Chandler. These two locations are where the friends get to touch base in all the busyness of their city lives. They keep up with the news over a cup of coffee, living out of one another's pockets in apartments that are situated close together.

In *The One With Ross's Inappropriate Song*, Joey thinks about buying Monica's ex-boyfriend Richard's apartment. Richard, much to Chandler's annoyance, is evidently moving up in the world. Meanwhile, Phoebe is going to meet her new boyfriend's parents. Their backgrounds could not be more diverse – she used to live on the street, they are among New York's finest and richest. Phoebe changes her clothes and her accent to try and fit in, but cannot hide the truth.

Key Issue: Living in the City

It is hard to imagine *Friends* set anywhere else but in New York. The apartments and coffee houses are essential backdrops, while the friends' lives are defined by the opportunities they grab in the metropolis. They create a mutual reference point for each other in the middle of the diversity and energy that is city. They embrace city life enthusiastically, and enjoy its advantages. Those of us watching who live in cities may well identify with their approach, or perhaps envy the success they seem to make of it. While the vast majority of us live in towns or cities in the West, we all know that the reality of city life is not just fun and games. So can the Bible help us with living in the city? Does it see cities as good or bad? What about the mixed cultures they attract, and the energy they generate? What is the city for?

Bible Study

Choose one question from each section. There is some progression in the second questions of each section – focusing on Babylon in the Old and New Testaments and contrasting this with the new Jerusalem. You may like to do all these questions although they can be taken individually.

1. Self-sufficiency

Chandler: ***So how come Richard's selling the place? Went bankrupt? Medical malpractice? Choked on his own moustache?***

Listing Agent: ***Actually, he is buying a much bigger place. It's got a great view of Central Pa—***

Chandler: ***(interrupting) Mmm, that's enough about you!***

◆ Read Genesis 11:1–9. Why did the men think they would be better off in a city with a big tower? Why did God stop them?

◆ Read Daniel 4:4–37. Why was Nebuchadnezzar so pleased with himself? How did his perspectives on his city and kingdom change?

2. Diversity

Phoebe: ***Listen! You have to help me pick a dress 'cause I'm meeting Mike's parents tonight!***

Monica: ***Wow, the boyfriend's parents! That's a big step.***

Phoebe: (sarcastically) ***Really? That hadn't occurred to me.***

Monica: ***They just gonna love you, just be yourself.***

Phoebe: ***They live on the Upper East Side on Park Avenue!***

Rachel: ***Oh yeah, she can't be herself.***

◆ Read Acts 18:1–17. How did Paul relate to the different kinds of people in Corinth? How did the spread of the Gospel benefit from this diversity?

See also 1 Corinthians 10:23–11:1.

◆ Read Revelation 18:1–20. What kinds of people and activities did this city attract? Was this diversity all bad?

Leaders: This passage draws on Old Testament references to Babylon and uses it as a metaphor to represent the satanic system of evil that has corrupted history. Much of the diversity of the city in this passage is, therefore, expressed negatively. It is a continuation of the announcement of the judgment on the prostitute of Revelation 17. It is likely that the city of Rome is mainly in view (compare 17:19).

3. Energy

Look at this place. Why am I so intimidated by this guy? Pretentious art, this huge macho couch. When we know all he does is sit around all day crying about losing Monica to a real man! ... You don't think he's here, do you? (Chandler, in Richard's apartment)

◆ Acts 19:23–41. What impact did the Gospel have on the city of Ephesus? How does the vitality of the city rise and fall in this passage?

◆ Read Revelation 18:11–24. How is the vitality of the city expressed before judgment falls on it? What are the positive and negative aspects of this?

4. Refuge

Originally I'm from upstate, but ... then my mom killed herself and my step dad went to prison, so ... I just moved to the city where um ... I actually lived in a burned out Buick LeSabre for a while ... which was okay, that was okay, until um ... I got hepatitis, you know, 'cause this pimp spit in my mouth and ... but I ... I got over it and um ... Anyway, now I'm um ... a freelance massage therapist, hm ... which, you know, isn't always steady money but at least I don't pay taxes, ... (Phoebe)

◆ Read Psalm 87. Why is Zion a place of safety and rejoicing? Who is God calling into this refuge?

Leaders: Rahab (87:4) represents Egypt (see also Isaiah 30:7) – the reference is to a sea monster called Rahab rather than to the woman in Joshua 2. This Psalm is looking forward to the ultimate fulfilment of God's promise to restore Jerusalem. God's purposes have always been broader than simply Israel and here he is promising that people from pagan nations will also have a place in this great fulfilment. See also Isaiah 2:2–4.

◆ Read Revelation 21:9–27. In what ways is this city the ultimate refuge? If it is a refuge, why do the gates never get shut (21:25)?

See also Numbers 35:1–13

Implications

You know, all Phoebe has done tonight is trying to get you to like her. And maybe that hasn't been clear all the time, but she did her best. And yeah – she's a little different than you are. (Mike, Phoebe's boyfriend, to his parents)

Choose one or more of the following questions.

◆ What do you think about your nearest city? Do you think you have attitudes to it that God would like to change? How could you make city life better for others?

◆ Are you a self-sufficient person? When is this a good thing and when does this get in the way of your relationship with God?

◆ What would you say to someone who contends that humankind is truly self-sufficient and does not need God?

◆ What do you understand about the heavenly city that awaits us at the end of all things? What are you looking forward to?

◆ What would you say to a young person who aspires to move to the big city and adopt the *Friends* way of life?

Prayer

Spend some time praying through these issues.

Background Reading

You will find links to some background reading on the Connect Bible Studies website: www.connectbiblestudies.com

Discuss

Discuss this study in the online discussion forums at www.connectbiblestudies.com

Members' Sheet: Friends – Part 2

Summary

New York – the ultimate high-rise, high-living city. Somewhere in Manhattan there is a corner that is home to six friends. They all have their own reasons for ending up in the city, but share a love for the place that has offered them so much. New York has got room for Ross the palaeontologist, Phoebe the masseuse, Joey the actor – and there is always opportunity for growth. Rachel transformed herself from a waitress into a fashion industry executive. When she first arrived in New York, Rachel couldn't even do her own washing. Over the last ten years her confidence has grown and now she is the independent woman of her dreams.

Most of the action takes place in or between the 'Central Perk' coffee house and Monica's apartment, which she now shares with husband Chandler. These two locations are where the friends get to touch base in all the busyness of their city lives. They keep up with the news over a cup of coffee, living out of one another's pockets in apartments that are situated close together.

In *The One With Ross's Inappropriate Song*, Joey thinks about buying Monica's ex-boyfriend Richard's apartment. Richard, much to Chandler's annoyance, is evidently moving up in the world. Meanwhile, Phoebe is going to meet her new boyfriend's parents. Their backgrounds could not be more diverse – she used to live on the street, they are among New York's finest and richest. Phoebe changes her clothes and her accent to try and fit in, but cannot hide the truth.

Key Issue

Bible Study notes

Implications

Prayer

Discuss this study in the online discussion forums at www.connectbiblestudies.com

14

Friends

Warner Bros.

Part Three: Generation X

Amy: ***You don't want me to be happy. You ... you have always been jealous of me.***

Rachel: ***Jealous of what? Of your lack of responsibility? Your immaturity? Your total disregard of other people's feelings?***

Please read Using Connect Bible Studies *(page 3) before leading a Bible study using this material.*

Opening Questions

Choose one of these questions.

What are the characteristics of your generation?	What characteristics of *Friends* are typical of Generation X?
How would you define Generation X?	Do you think Western culture is progressing or deteriorating? Why?

Summary

So no one told you life was gonna be this way
Your job's a joke, you're broke, your love life's D.O.A. ...
I'll be there for you, 'cause you're there for me too
(*Friends'* title theme, by the Rembrandts)

When family breaks down, who do Generation Xers turn to? Their friends, of course. Traumas from childhood recur for all of the friends (except perhaps for Joey – the only one with a strong and reasonably stable family background) and spill over into every part of their lives. Community and relationship matter to the Gen X friends, but these things are found in the friendships they have chosen to forge, rather than in the family links that have always let them down.

Chandler carries the emotional scars of having a steamy novelist for a mother and a drag queen for a father; Monica is made to feel that she can never measure up to her mother – no matter what she does. The six friends represent a generation who don't see the old ways working and who don't want to turn into their parents.

In *The One With Rachel's Other Sister*, Rachel is confronted with a younger version of herself, who might be compared to the immature Rachel of the early days of *Friends*. Rachel invites Amy to spend Thanksgiving with the pseudo *Friends* family. Amy assumes that baby Emma would live with her, should parents Ross and Rachel die. Rachel is adamant that only her best friend Monica is responsible enough to be guardian.

Key Issue: Generation X

Initially coined by Douglas Coupland as the title for his book, the term Generation X has become a useful description for some and remains a complete mystery to others. It is defined by *Chambers Dictionary* as 'those sections of society that are sceptical about traditionally held beliefs and values, e.g. relating to work and the family.' Generation X describes those born between 1961 and 1980 – just the ages of the *Friends*. So the *Friends* lifestyles portray some of the Generation X characteristics. Many of us will also relate to the sense of isolation which comes from broken family backgrounds, or moving away from our roots. We too experience so much of life through the media, and we too face a multitude of life choices every day. Around us we see the fallout from a culture which finds it hard to make a commitment and stick to it. How can the Bible help us with the challenge of Generation X?

Bible Study

Choose one question from each section.

1. Disconnected Lives

Amy: **Why can't you ever be supportive?**
Rachel: **Supp— ... You want to talk supportive? You didn't even come and visit me when I was in the hospital having the baby.**
Amy: **Oh. Yeah. Well ... You didn't come see me when I was in the hospital when I was getting my lips done.**
Rachel: **I did the first time!**

◆ Read Mark 3:20–35. What had happened to Jesus' family relationships? Who was Jesus close to? Why?

◆ Read Luke 15:11–32. Why did these family relationships break down? How was reconciliation possible? Why was the older son not part of it?

2. Living in a media world

Amy: *Oh, I was just thinking. You know what would be incredible? If you guys died.*
Ross: *Thank you, Amy.*
Amy: *No, no, then I would get the baby. I mean, you know it would be just like a movie. Like at first I wouldn't know what to do with her, then I would rise to the occasion and then I would get a makeover and then I'd get married.*
Phoebe: *That's a great movie!*

◆ Read Daniel 1:1–21. What pressures was Daniel facing in his new situation? How did he respond?

◆ Read John 17:1–26. How does Jesus want us to relate to the world? Why?

3. Too much choice

Amy: *This might be my one chance to have a baby, Rachel. I mean, you know that I have been so busy focusing on my career.*
Rachel: *What? What career?*
Amy: *Um ... I'm a decorator.*
Rachel: *OK. You decorate dad's office and so now you're a decorator. OK! I went to the zoo yesterday and now I'm a koala bear.*

◆ Read Ecclesiastes 2:1–23. What did the Teacher gain by trying out so many different things? Why did he conclude that his choices were meaningless?

◆ Read Acts 17:16–34. What choices were on offer in Athenian society at the time? Why did Paul's message in the Areopagus provoke the responses seen in verse 32?

Leaders: The word 'babbler' in verse 18 literally means 'seed pecker'. It suggests that they thought Paul was combining bits and pieces from many sources.

4. Lack of commitment

My boyfriend cancelled on me. I mean ... I finally find a real relationship. I mean, someone that I can spend this day with and then his wife comes back into town. I swear, it's almost not worth dating married guys. (Amy)

◆ Read Hosea 2:2–23. How does Gomer's lack of commitment parallel the unfaithfulness of God's people? Why was commitment not important to her? How does God respond?

◆ Read 2 Timothy 4:1–22. How does Paul feel about his friends, especially those who showed a lack of commitment? What should Timothy do in the face of people's lack of commitment to the Gospel?

Implications

Ross and Rachel don't know what they're talking about. I mean, it's not like they're so responsible. Emma is a product of a bottle of Merlot, and a five-year-old condom.
(Monica)

Choose one or more of the following questions.

- ◆ Do you identify with the characteristics of Generation X? How can these characteristics – and you – be used in God's service?

- ◆ What are the painful areas in your family relationships? Do you have attitudes that need to change? How can God help?

- ◆ How much do you pick up your beliefs, values and attitudes from the media? Should this change? How?

- ◆ How would you talk to someone who seems to have given up on Jesus?

- ◆ What would you say to someone who is thinking of leaving their spouse because they 'don't want to be married any more'?

- ◆ Do you struggle with commitment? Why? How could God help you to change?

- ◆ What would you say to someone who disapproves of *Friends* casual approach to sex?

Prayer

Spend some time praying through these issues.

Background Reading

You will find links to some background reading on the Connect Bible Studies website: www.connectbiblestudies.com

Discuss

Discuss this study in the online discussion forums at www.connectbiblestudies.com

Members' Sheet: Friends – Part 3

Summary

So no one told you life was gonna be this way
Your job's a joke, you're broke, your love life's D.O.A. ...
I'll be there for you, 'cause you're there for me too
(*Friends'* title theme, by the Rembrandts)

When family breaks down, who do Generation Xers turn to? Their friends, of course. Traumas from childhood recur for all of the friends (except perhaps for Joey – the only one with a strong and reasonably stable family background) and spill over into every part of their lives. Community and relationship matter to the Gen X friends, but these things are found in the friendships they have chosen to forge, rather than in the family links that have always let them down.

Chandler carries the emotional scars of having a steamy novelist for a mother and a drag queen for a father; Monica is made to feel that she can never measure up to her mother – no matter what she does. The six friends represent a generation who don't see the old ways working and who don't want to turn into their parents.

In *The One With Rachel's Other Sister*, Rachel is confronted with a younger version of herself, who might be compared to the immature Rachel of the early days of *Friends*. Rachel invites Amy to spend Thanksgiving with the pseudo *Friends* family. Amy assumes that baby Emma would live with her, should parents Ross and Rachel die. Rachel is adamant that only her best friend Monica is responsible enough to be guardian.

Key Issue

Bible Study notes

Implications

Prayer

Discuss this study in the online discussion forums at www.connectbiblestudies.com

www.connectbiblestudies.com

connect

linking the Word to the world

Friends

Warner Bros.

Part Four: Longing

Rachel:	***Ross, could you stop by the coffee house and get me a muffin?***
Ross:	***Sure, what kind?***
Rachel:	***Umm, let me think ... What do I want? What ... do ... I ... want?***
Ross:	***Please take your time, it's an important decision. Not like, say ... I know – deciding to marry someone! This is about a muffin!***

Please read Using Connect Bible Studies *(page 3) before leading a Bible study using this material.*

Opening Questions

Choose one of these questions.

What was your greatest longing when you were a child?	Do you know what your greatest longings are now? Are there any you could share?
What do you think the *Friends* long for most?	Is longing for something good or bad? Why?

Summary

Throughout all nine series of *Friends*, the comedy of the show is underpinned by the heartfelt desires of each of the friends: Joey's pursuit of an acting career; Monica's desire to run her own restaurant; Rachel's urge to shop, shop and shop some more; or just the ongoing longing for romantic attachments that ebb and flow for each of the friends with predictable regularity.

Even when things are going well, it is rare for any of the friends to reach a state of contentment. There is always something missing, something to be sought that is just over the horizon and can't be found at the bottom of a coffee cup. Some of the deeper longings felt by the friends are related to problems of the past: Phoebe doesn't want to feel like an outsider; Chandler just wants to be a regular guy; Ross would like people to find him interesting.

In *The One Where Emma Cries*, Rachel is so desperate to spend time with her new baby that she wakes Emma up in the middle of her sleep. Everyone just wants the baby to stop crying. Chandler is also suffering from lack of sleep – his longing to make a good impression at an important meeting means that he cannot sleep for worrying. Unfortunately, the next day he nods off at a crucial point. When he wakes up, he unwittingly agrees to a promotion that entails moving to Tulsa. The news does not go down well with his wife, Monica.

Key Issue: Longing

Perhaps one reason for the success of *Friends* is the way the characters chase the same dreams that we do. Much of the humour, and the storyline, revolve around the search for meaningful relationships and resulting happiness. There can't be many of us who have not got caught up in that one. Then New York offers a bewildering variety of material comforts to covet – which of us would turn them down? The *Friends* are constantly trying to sort out their lives to bring in a bit of stability, and every so often hint at a bigger, deep down longing for spiritual significance to their lives. So what does the Bible say about our longings for security and comfort, and for relationships with each other and God?

Bible Study

Choose one question from each section.

1. Longing for material comfort

Chandler: *You know how we always said that it would be fun to move to Paris for a year? You know, you could study French cooking and I could write and we could take a picnic along the Seine and go wine tasting in Bordeaux?*

Monica: *Oh yeah* (smiles).

Chandler: *OK, you know that people say that Tulsa is the Paris of Oklahoma?*

Monica: *What? Who says that?*

Chandler: *People who've never ever been to Paris.*

Monica: *What's going on?*

Chandler: *We're moving to Tulsa!*

◆　Read Ecclesiastes 5:8–6:12. Why does material comfort not necessarily bring satisfaction? What are the advantages of being poor?

◆　Read Luke 12:13–34. What do people gain by seeking material comfort? Why did Jesus warn against this? What do people gain by seeking God's kingdom?

2. Longing for significance

Monica: *All right, not that this matters, but did they at least offer you a huge raise?*

Chandler: *No, no, but they are going to lease us a Ford Focus.* (**Monica's not impressed.**) *I'll get out of it.*

◆ Read 1 Samuel 18:1–19. What did Saul and David depend on for their sense of significance? How did this affect their behaviour?

◆ Read Mark 12:38–44. What contrast did Mark draw in these two incidents? How did Jesus measure significance?

3. Longing for love and relationships

Ross: *You said you'd marry Joey?*
Rachel: *OK, you have to realise, I was exhausted, I was emotional, I would have said yes to anybody. Like that time you and I got married ... I'm not helping.*

◆ Read Ecclesiastes 4:7–12. Why is a life of isolation meaningless? What difference do relationships make?

◆ Read John 4:4–29. What did this woman want out of life? How did Jesus speak to her deepest needs?

4. Longing for God

Rachel: *You know what? I can't even worry about that right now, cause I got the cutie little baby. Oh, I can't believe how much I love her – I can't get enough of her! Like right now I miss her, I actually miss her.*
Phoebe: **(Pointing to the baby)** *You know, that's ... that's her.*

◆ Read Psalm 84:1–12. How does the Psalmist express his longing for God? How does God satisfy this longing?

◆ Read John 6:25–59. Why does Jesus use the metaphor of bread here? How does he satisfy our deepest longings?

Implications

Rachel: *You have got to get over this Joey thing, OK? I never really wanted to marry Joey, OK?*
Ross: *OK.*
Rachel: *You know what I really, really want?*
Ross: *What, Rach?*
Rachel: *I wanna sleep, I wanna eat, I wanna take a shower – I mean before she wakes up and we gotta do this all over again.*

Choose one or more of the following questions.

◆ What are your biggest longings in life? Do you share them with God?

- Is the longing for personal significance universal? Are you aware of it in yourself? How can you let God satisfy that longing?

- Do you trust that God is enough for you? Why/why not?

- What would you say to someone who desperately wants a romantic relationship, so they can be happy?

- What would you say to someone who asks if God could make them happy?

- Why do so many people long for and pursue material comfort?

- Are you happy with your attitude to material comfort? Why/why not? What can you do about it?

- King David wrote psalms, played the lyre and danced. How do you express your longing for God? How do you experience his presence?

Prayer

Spend some time praying through these issues.

Background Reading

You will find links to some background reading on the Connect Bible Studies website: www.connectbiblestudies.com

Discuss

Discuss this study in the online discussion forums at www.connectbiblestudies.com

Members' Sheet: Friends – Part 4

Summary

Throughout all nine series of *Friends*, the comedy of the show is underpinned by the heartfelt desires of each of the friends: Joey's pursuit of an acting career; Monica's desire to run her own restaurant; Rachel's urge to shop, shop and shop some more; or just the ongoing longing for romantic attachments that ebb and flow for each of the friends with predictable regularity.

Even when things are going well, it is rare for any of the friends to reach a state of contentment. There is always something missing, something to be sought that is just over the horizon and can't be found at the bottom of a coffee cup. Some of the deeper longings felt by the friends are related to problems of the past: Phoebe doesn't want to feel like an outsider; Chandler just wants to be a regular guy; Ross would like people to find him interesting.

In *The One Where Emma Cries*, Rachel is so desperate to spend time with her new baby that she wakes Emma up in the middle of her sleep. Everyone just wants the baby to stop crying. Chandler is also suffering from lack of sleep – his longing to make a good impression at an important meeting means that he cannot sleep for worrying. Unfortunately, the next day he nods off at a crucial point. When he wakes up, he unwittingly agrees to a promotion that entails moving to Tulsa. The news does not go down well with his wife, Monica.

Key Issue

Bible Study notes

Implications

Prayer

Discuss this study in the online discussion forums at www.connectbiblestudies.com